We sh ll
be changed

We shall
be changed

An Lent Course in the Celtic Tradition

Keith Duke

First published in 2004 by
KEVIN MAYHEW LTD
Buxhall, Stowmarket, Suffolk, IP14 3BW
E-mail: info@kevinmayhewltd.com

9 8 7 6 5 4 3 2 1 0

ISBN 1 84417 328 3
Catalogue No. 1500743

Cover design by Angela Selfe
Edited and Typeset by Graham Harris

Printed and bound in Great Britain

CONTENTS

ACKNOWLEDGEMENTS

My special thanks to Val Whitaker, who has read through all this material at its different stages of development and who always made constructive suggestions for its improvement; and to Anna Leggett at Kevin Mayhew for her support and co-operation.

Many thanks to the following for permission for me to use their copyright material:
Ken Wilber, *One Taste*; Rosa Romani, *Green Spirituality*; Hugh McGregor Ross, *Jesus Untouched by the Church*; Neil Douglas-Klotz, *The Hidden Gospel*; Glennie Kindred, *Sacred Celebrations*; Wendell Berry, *Circles*; Andy Baggott, *The Celtic Wheel of Life*; Robert van de Weyer, *Celtic Fire*; Michael Mitton, *Restoring the Woven Cord*.

INTRODUCTION

The doorway into the music room was wide enough for a wheelchair and high enough for a double bass – and S filled it. He was a big lad with a big personality and a seemingly big grudge against the world in general and school in particular.

Lessons were always difficult, particularly as he was in a 'hard' group who thrived on his seemingly rude and outlandish behaviour. There was no point in getting cross with S – he just laughed at you. There was no point in sending him out – he just came back. There was no point in trying to argue with him – he always thought he was right. He had the ability to come up with a devastating quip that would put you down and make him look good. I eventually left the school – and teaching – but went back for a presentation evening where a seemingly even larger S came up, shook my hand, asked me how I was and, in his own inimitable way, said thanks for putting up with him. There had clearly been some form of change in S at the deepest level.

Alex, the lead character in the film *A Clockwork Orange*, is vicious, violent and completely amoral. Following a series of rapes and other violent incidents, he is attacked by his associates after murdering a woman and is consequently caught by the police.

While in prison, he is befriended by the chaplain and becomes a model prisoner, and eventually volunteers for a new kind of aversion therapy being tried out in various prisons. The Minister for the Interior openly promises that 'this vicious young hoodlum will be transformed out of all recognition' to such a degree that he will never offend again.

After the treatment, the prison chaplain is critical of the effects, on the grounds that Alex 'ceases being a creature capable of moral choice'. Effectively, he suggests, Alex has not inwardly changed – it's only fear of physical pain that prevents him from responding violently or touching a woman.

Both characters in these tales experienced some kind of trans-formation – Alex through fear, S through experiencing patience, gentleness and a genuine belief that he had something to offer. Too often changes in attitudes and behaviour are based upon fear. Fear of damnation, fear of not belonging, fear of getting it wrong or fear of not coping with life.

This course aims to develop an open understanding of transformation and how it affects our spiritual journey. I work on the assumption that transformation is personal and grounded in a developing relationship with God – not some kind of training or therapy that carries someone else's agenda. At times we will need to take risks that threaten our comfort, but often this is the only way to approach an understanding and knowing within ourselves that changes us at the deepest level.

Keith Duke, August 2004

NOTES FOR LEADERS

Encouraging others to come forward:

A course in five parts is an excellent opportunity for five different people (or pairs of people?) to lead a session each, and, unless it's absolutely unavoidable, an opportunity for the usual organiser to take a back seat! So if you're the priest/vicar, worship leader, or whatever, this is your time to be 'done unto'. So make the most of it – it probably doesn't happen that often!

The leader's role is simply to help each session move along within the allotted time. This will happen more easily if you:
- know the material well by thoroughly reading the course, or at least your part of it;
- be aware of the resources needed and have them readily available;
- make sure the group knows exactly what to do and how much time they have to do it;
- give opportunities for everyone to contribute;
- gently hold back those who tend to dominate the discussion, whoever they are!
- don't expect to be perfect – nobody is, however good they might seem!

Each session requires the following:
- a copy of this booklet for each person involved;
- a good supply of paper, pens, pencils, etc., so participants can make notes;
- a flipchart or large sheets of paper and large pens to record the points shared in the feedback sessions;
- song words and a musician with instrument if you intend to sing (or CD and player);
- refreshments with someone else designated to prepare and serve them.

You might need:

- bread and wine in suitable containers if you intend to share the Eucharist at the end of the session;
- CD and/or tape player with suitably gentle instrumental music;
- visual materials, anything that will help illustrate the content of the course;
- candles, matches, incense, textiles, stones, etc., that will help create a prayerful space, especially if you wish to include a time of open prayer.
- and to ensure group comfort try to use a space that will not be overcrowded and has comfortable chairs.

Bible sources are at the beginning of each session. Encourage your group to read each one beforehand so that they are not approaching the session cold. All the gospel references include chapter and verse to enable those taking part to use other translations during the course, or to look up the references at their leisure. However, it's worth encouraging your group to read the whole chapter and to see the quotation in its full context.

The structure of each session is the same, but it can be adjusted according to circumstances. Opportunities are given for Welcome and Feedback at each session, but keep these brief. The periods of silence are important, as they allow people to reflect more deeply on the discussion and organise or store thoughts before moving on.

The initial Group Exploration of each session is designed to look in detail at specific areas of transformation, often through gospel and other stories. The second Individual or Paired Reflection is designed to work more intimately at ways of applying this learning.

The format of breaking down into small groups and then feeding back to the whole group does allow people to consider a greater variety of views than when working as a whole, as well as allowing those who are more nervous to contribute.

How you organise this will depend on the total number of participants and their experience of working in this way. Each session features an Other Activity – a song, poem, video clip, drama or visual material. Use this time creatively – sing as a group or have one person share a song, poem or painting, or whatever, that is relevant to the session.

The Opening and Closing Worship is a vital part of each session. A time of open prayer could also be included, but specific prayer time is not listed within the sessions as many groups run a Lent course in addition to their regular prayer events. You might want to share bread and wine at the end of the final session.

Please use the Liturgies in this booklet. They may be unfamiliar at first, since they have been created in the Celtic tradition, but their value lies in their simplicity and challenge. When blessing and sharing Communion, your church tradition may require that you have a priest to do this. But you can choose a leader from the group to pass bread and wine around the circle, each person adding a blessing of their own to that already given by the leader. Feel free to use any of these liturgies elsewhere.

Songs and recordings have been suggested because they reflect the content of the course and are very accessible. Contact Kevin Mayhew Ltd on 01449 737978 for CDs, or order via the website *<www.kevinmayhewltd.com>*

Finally, encourage members of the group to be creative. There is a wealth of poets, composers, songwriters, painters, photographers, sculptors, dancers, actors, playwrights and performance artists who create wondrous things. We need new hymns, songs, poems, prayers, sketches and images that reflect the new understandings we have of the gospel and spiritual journeying. Encourage the group to go for it, and to share what they create with others!

OPENING THOUGHTS

Why should we believe?

Believe nothing, O monks, merely because you have been told it . . .
   or because it is traditional,
   or because you yourselves have imagined it.
Do not believe what your teacher tells you
   merely out of respect for the teacher.
But whatsoever, after due examination and analysis,
   you find to be conducive to the good,
   the benefit, the welfare of all beings,
   that doctrine believe and cling to, and take it as your guide.

Buddha

The choice is ours

What does God want? Does God want goodness or the choice of
goodness? Is a man who chooses the bad perhaps in some way
better than a man who has the good imposed on him?

Anthony Burgess, from A Clockwork Orange

SESSION 1 – WHAT IS TRANSFORMATION?

Meeting outline for Session 1

Welcome

Opening worship (see page 33)

Silence

Group exploration

- ▸ What is Transformation? How would you decide whether or not an experience is truly transformational? (Sources A and C).
- ▸ How might we develop a more spiritual and transformative approach in our lives? (Sources B, D and E).

Feedback from group exploration

Silence

Other activity

- ▸ Song, poem, video clip, drama or visual material relevant to this session.

Individual or paired reflection:

- ▸ Examine events you have seen or experienced in your lifetime that are transformational. Which of these seemed sudden (a vision, a sudden dawning of an idea, a releasing of a prejudice or belief) and which seemed to take longer (a gradual realisation, a gentle change of direction)? Which of these seemed to create a more fundamental change? Why?

Feedback from reflection

Silence

Closing worship (see page 34)

SOURCE A – Matthew 7:7-8

Jesus said: 'Ask and it will be given to you; seek and you will find; knock and the door will be opened to you. For everyone who asks receives; he who seeks finds; and to him who knocks, the door will be opened.'

When we consciously commit ourselves to a goal, in prayer, meditation or action, we make a spiritual statement. We are leaving space for the One to speak to us through whatever happens in the course of our meditation or endeavour. Ask, seek and knock in Aramaic, reflect the sense of creating space with sincere intensity. All of the results of these efforts (given, find and opened) in Aramaic, emphasise processes of nature that happen easily, such as a loving action or a natural response to something that has already happened. When we work up the passion to follow something wholeheartedly, we blow into life the fire of love within us. This devotion, rather than the object we pursue, is the real goal. In the end, it doesn't so much matter where we start as that we start. Holiness is about wholeness.

Neil Douglas-Klotz reflecting on Matthew 7:7-8

SOURCE B – The Gospel of Thomas, Saying 2

Jesus said: 'Let him who seeks not cease from seeking until he finds; and when he finds, he will be turned around, and when he is turned around he will marvel and he shall reign over the All.'

In the commentary on this, and other sayings in the Gospel of Thomas, Hugh McGregor Ross comments that this turning around 'may be no more than a pool of clear water in a mountain stream being stirred'. More often it involves leaving behind old luggage from previous teachings.

SOURCE C – Transformation

Even though English dictionaries differ slightly in their definition of the word transformation, they all agree that it involves some kind of radical or complete change, usually for the better. This definition may also include conversion, metamorphosis, renewal and transfiguration that are often seen as part of the transformational process.

In the excellent introduction to her book *Green Spirituality*, Rosa Romani explores two contrasting experiences of the Divine that she calls religion and spirituality. She sees religion as:

'Something that has been fashioned by men, for men. A construction that categorically answers a basic human need for meaning. It is a fixed proposition that promotes an unshakeable adherence; it is not about resurgence or growth in a natural verdant sense but about continuity and steadiness. It has little of the spontaneity or unpredictability of a living spirituality; rather it is a rigid structure that shelters us from other more refined ways of being. It has been domesticated and certainly won't do anything astonishing.'

Rosa Romani also recognises that within the religious experience, we hand over our autonomy to the belief system, and, in doing so, we become roped together like people climbing a mountain – a chain of command that eventually connects us to the Divine. Again, there is the suggestion that this experience makes life safer and easier for us since it provides all the answers to our questions, and gives us clear boundaries for our beliefs and experiences. She sees spirituality as:

'Everything to do with individual exploration and personal feelings; an experiential way in which we can feed directly from that which is sacred in order to reach our fullest potential and so blossom accordingly. Spirituality is more about having an active faith in the existence of the sacred than in a hard and fast belief in it and a desire to label it conclusively. Faith, perhaps, is about hope and searching whilst religious belief already knows and feels safe to shut the door on other possibilities. When we believe in a religious sense, we are all too ready to draw lines in the sand which say "us and them" or "right and wrong". Such divisions are the tools of separation, not of ongoing transformation.'

In his book *One Taste*, Ken Wilber goes further and sees our experiences as both translative and transformative. The translative, he feels:

'. . . acts as a way of creating meaning: it offers myths and stories and tales and narratives and rituals and revivals that, taken together, help us make sense of, and endure, the slings and arrows of outrageous fortune. This function of religion does not usually or necessarily change the level of consciousness in a person.'

In effect, Ken Wilber says this experience is concerned with providing a place of safety and consolation by the self being given a new way to think about the world. The transformative experience, however:

'. . . does not fortify the self, but shatters it; is not consolation but devastation; is not complacency but explosion; is not comfort but revolution.'

Although both Ken Wilber and Rosa Romani recognise that safe translative or religious experiences play an essential part in our development, they both feel that only the more inner spiritual journeying can be truly transformative in the way that Jesus, and other spiritual teachers suggest.

SOURCE D – The inner world

We have been taught to fear our inner world and to mistrust the information we may receive through insights, intuition and our connection to our own inherent wisdom. We need to understand our unconscious selves, and to learn to listen to our inner voice. We can use the energy of the dark time of the year to explore these inner parts. Turn and look at what you fear, and the understanding this brings. Seek the truth in the darkness, look for ways to find the Divine within. Out of a difficult situation comes power, hope, rebirth, inner strength, wisdom and maturity.

Glennie Kindred

SOURCE E – The Celtic path

What does one need to follow the Celtic path? Firstly, you need a deep-rooted faith, a belief that you are on this planet to learn and grow as spiritual beings and that you are responsible for everything that manifests in your life.

Secondly, you need doubt! How can you have faith and doubt? The doubt I am talking about is a sense of being ever questioning: Why is there so much suffering in the world? What can I do to change that? What are the lessons I need to understand? Without doubt, without a questioning mind, you will never find the happiness we all seek.

Thirdly, you need determination, a determination to keep searching for answers until all doubt is gone from your mind, a determination to find the answers to every question your mind can create.

Andy Baggott

SESSION 2 – ISSUES OF CLEANLINESS

Meeting outline for Session 2

Welcome

Opening worship (see page 33)

Silence

Group exploration
> ‣ How did Jesus break the Law of Moses by healing the woman 'subject to bleeding' and Jairus' daughter? How did this affect Jesus' ability to minister to these women? (Sources F, H and I).
> ‣ What were the potentially transforming lessons for the woman 'subject to bleeding', Jairus (an official at the temple) and the onlookers (especially in relation to Jesus' statement from the Gospel of Thomas in source G)?
> ‣ How does the story of John of Beverley suggest we approach healing? Does this have a message for us today?

Feedback from group exploration

Silence

Other activity
> ‣ Song, poem, section of video, drama or visual material relevant to this session.

Individual or paired reflection
> ‣ Examine the role of healing in your personal journey. How do you wish to develop this? Are there barriers that prevent you developing this aspect of your ministry?

Feedback from reflection

Silence

Closing worship (see page 34)

SOURCE F – Luke 8:40-56

Now when Jesus returned, a crowd welcomed him, for they were all expecting him. Then a man named Jairus, a ruler of the synagogue, came and fell at Jesus' feet, pleading with him to come to his house because his only daughter, a girl of about 12, was dying. As Jesus was on his way, the crowds almost crushed him.

And a woman was there who had been subject to bleeding for 12 years, but no one could heal her. She came up behind him and touched the edge of his cloak, and immediately her bleeding stopped.

'Who touched me?' Jesus asked.

When they all denied it, Peter said, 'Master, the people are crowding and pressing against you.'

But Jesus said, 'Someone touched me; I know that power has gone out from me.' Then the woman, seeing that she could not go unnoticed, came trembling and fell at his feet. In the presence of all the people, she told why she had touched him and how she had been instantly healed.

Then he said to her, 'Daughter, your faith has healed you. Go in peace.'

While Jesus was still speaking, someone came from the house of Jairus, the synagogue ruler.

'Your daughter is dead,' he said. 'Don't bother the teacher any more.'

Hearing this, Jesus said to Jairus, 'Don't be afraid; just believe, and she will be healed.'

When he arrived at the house of Jairus, he did not let anyone go in with him except Peter, John and James, and the child's father and mother.

Meanwhile, all the people were wailing and mourning for her.

'Stop wailing,' Jesus said. 'She is not dead but asleep.'

They laughed at him, knowing that she was dead. But he took her by the hand and said, 'My child, get up!' Her spirit returned, and at once she stood up. Then Jesus told them to give her something to eat. Her parents were astonished, but he ordered them not to tell anyone what had happened.

SOURCE G – The Gospel of Thomas, saying 66

Jesus said, 'Show me the stone the builders have rejected: it is that, the corner-stone.'

SOURCE H – Leviticus 15:19-30

When a woman has her regular flow of blood, the impurity of her monthly period will last seven days, and anyone who touches her will be unclean till evening.

Anything she lies on during her period will be unclean, and anything she sits on will be unclean. Whoever touches her bed must wash his clothes and bathe with water, and he will be unclean till evening. Whoever touches anything she sits on must wash his clothes and bathe with water, and he will be unclean till evening. Whether it is the bed or anything she was sitting on, when anyone touches it, he will be unclean till evening.

If a man lies with her and her monthly flow touches him, he will be unclean for seven days; any bed he lies on will be unclean. When a woman has a discharge of blood for many days at a time other than her monthly period or has a discharge that continues beyond her period, she will be unclean as long as she has the discharge, just as in the days of her period.

SOURCE I – Numbers 19:11-12

Anyone who touches a dead person's body will be unclean for seven days. He must make himself clean with special water. He must do it on the third day. He must also do it on the seventh day. Then he will be clean.

SOURCE J – John of Beverley

In AD 685, a man known as John of Beverley was made Bishop of Hexham. By any reckoning he was a remarkable person, overflowing with the Holy Spirit in such abundance that miracles featured fairly regularly in his ministry. A key to this was his custom of taking time away from his active ministry to reflect and pray. Bede tells us that 'whenever opportunity offers, and especially during Lent, this man of God used to retire with a few companions to read and pray quietly in an isolated house surrounded by open woodland and a dyke.' This was about a mile away from the church at Hexham, across the river Tyne. One spring John came here with his companions for his Lenten retreat and, as was his custom, he sent his companions to go and find some person in need whom they could invite to spend Lent with them in this little prayerful community. When this group went out, they came to a village where they found a dumb youth, whom John had already met on his visits here. This poor boy was not only afflicted with dumbness, but he also had a serious skin disease, which was so bad on his scalp that he had lost most of his hair. The boy gladly agreed to come and join the community for Lent.

After about a week John decided it was time to begin helping this lad, so he called him and asked him to stick out his tongue and show it to him. The boy duly obeyed, and John gently held his chin and then made the sign of the cross on his tongue. 'Now say a word; say yes,' he said, and the amazed boy found he could say 'yes'. Then, slowly and painstakingly, John went through the alphabet, helping him to pronounce all the letters. He taught him many words, all of which the boy delighted to learn. Eventually, the boy was saying full sentences. The floodgates were open and the boy did not stop talking, all the rest of the day and all night! Bede remarks that he was like the lame man healed by Peter and John, who could not stop walking and leaping and praising God. In the same way this boy delighted in his new found healing.

But the boy still had his terrible skin problem. For this, John decided to consult a doctor and 'with the assistance of the Bishop's blessing and prayers', the skin healed and new hair started to grow back on his head. By Easter day, a very happy young lad left this community, with clear skin, a fine head of hair and fluent in speech.

Michael Mitton

SESSION 3 – DESERT WATERS

Meeting outline for Session 3

Welcome

Opening worship (see page 33)

Silence

Group exploration
- ▸ Why do you think Jesus needed to spend time in the desert? (Sources K and M).
- ▸ What situations in our lives and journey could be regarded as deserts? (Sources M and N).
- ▸ In which ways can a desert experience make a transformational experience more likely? (Sources K, M and N).
- ▸ What does Jesus' saying from the gospel of Thomas suggest might be the first step in our journey of transformation? (Source L). What does that require of us?

Feedback from group exploration

Silence

Other activity
- ▸ Song, poem, video clip, drama or visual material relevant to this session.

Individual or paired reflection
- ▸ Examine your personal 'desert' experiences? Were they difficult to manage? What did you learn about yourself?

Feedback from reflection

Silence

Closing worship (see page 34)

SOURCE K – Matthew 4:1-11

Then Jesus was led by the Spirit into the desert to be tempted by the devil. After fasting forty days and forty nights, he was hungry. The tempter came to him and said, 'If you are the Son of God, tell these stones to become bread.' Jesus answered, 'It is written: "Man does not live on bread alone, but on every word that comes from the mouth of God."' Then the devil took him to the holy city and had him stand on the highest point of the temple. 'If you are the Son of God,' he said, 'throw yourself down. For it is written: "He will command his angels concerning you, and they will lift you up in their hands, so that you will not strike your foot against a stone."' Jesus answered him, 'It is also written: "Do not put the Lord your God to the test."' Again, the devil took him to a very high mountain and showed him all the kingdoms of the world and their splendour. 'All this I will give you,' he said, 'if you will bow down and worship me.' Jesus said to him, 'Away from me, Satan! For it is written: "Worship the Lord your God, and serve him only."' Then the devil left him, and angels came and attended him.

SOURCE L – Gospel of Thomas, saying 3

Jesus said, 'If those who guide your Being say to you behold the Kingdom is in the heaven, then the birds of the sky will precede you. If they say to you it is in the sea, then the fish will precede you. But the Kingdom is in your centre and is about you.

'When you Know your Selves then you will be Known, and you will be aware that you are the sons of the living Father. But if you do not Know yourselves then you are in poverty, and you are poverty.'

SOURCE M – *Desert Waters*

Why have I been drawn to this arid wilderness,
    this austere wasteland?
Why have I been drawn to this quiet solitude,
    this emptiness untouched by the material world?
Why have I been drawn to this desolate void,
    this destroyer of both comfort and security?

They tell me Jesus came here
    to pray,
    to face deep conflicts,
    to travel deeper into an understanding of self,
    to find the deepest presence
    and closest knowing of God.

Be still.
Do not be afraid.
Here, with searching,
    and careful discernment
    can be found all you need
    to satisfy your demanding body,
    your enquiring mind
    and your inner yearning
    to have your soul
    at one with God.
Only here can you become truly radical;
    only here can you return to the original rhythm
    that is Creation itself.

SOURCE N – *The Celtic Path*

What the Celtic path has taught me is to embrace everything with pleasure. Even when you are at your weakest and most disempowered, you can still relish the experience safe in the knowledge that you will emerge stronger and wiser because of it.

To understand strength, you must first experience weakness. To understand joy, you must first experience pain. Neither is good or bad until you choose how you interact with it. The Celtic path provides an understanding of how processes of learning unfold, allowing one to embrace change rather than fight it.

Andy Baggott

25

SESSION 4 – BEING BORN AGAIN

Meeting outline for Session 4

Welcome

Opening worship (see page 33)

Silence

Group exploration
> What do you think Jesus means by being born again? Is this the same as being transformed? (Sources O and P).
> Is this being born again a single event or a series of events? (Sources O, P and Q).
> Read Source Q to each other four or five times. How does this repetition help you understand its meaning?

Feedback from group exploration

Silence

Other activity
> Song, poem, video clip, drama or visual material relevant to this session.

Individual or paired reflection
> In which ways do you consider yourself to be born again? Where have you experienced a rebirth or transformation in your spiritual journey? Has this been related to revisiting familiar events such as Holy Week or Easter?

Feedback from reflection

Silence

Closing worship (see page 34)

SOURCE O – John 3:1-12

Now there was a man of the Pharisees named Nicodemus, a member of the Jewish ruling council. He came to Jesus at night and said, 'Rabbi, we know you are a teacher who has come from God. For no one could perform the miraculous signs you are doing if God were not with him.'

In reply Jesus declared, 'I tell you the truth, no one can see the kingdom of God unless he is born again.'

'How can a man be born when he is old?' Nicodemus asked. 'Surely he cannot enter a second time into his mother's womb to be born!'

Jesus answered, 'I tell you the truth, no one can enter the kingdom of God unless he is born of water and the Spirit. Flesh gives birth to flesh, but the Spirit gives birth to spirit. You should not be surprised at my saying, "You must be born again." The wind blows wherever it pleases. You hear its sound, but you cannot tell where it comes from or where it is going. So it is with everyone born of the Spirit.'

'How can this be?' Nicodemus asked.

'You are Israel's teacher,' said Jesus, 'and do you not understand these things? I tell you the truth, we speak of what we know, and we testify to what we have seen, but still you people do not accept our testimony. I have spoken to you of earthly things and you do not believe; how then will you believe if I speak of heavenly things?'

For 'born again', the Aramaic uses the words *min d'rish* – be born from the beginning. The word for water uses the same form as Genesis 1:2, which also means the flowing chaotic darkness. The Aramaic word for spirit can also mean breath. These clues show that Jesus advocated that Nicodemus recreate the creation story within himself by returning to the primordial darkness from which light first arose, using his own spirit-breath as a vehicle.

Neil Douglas-Klotz reflecting on John 3:1-12

SOURCE P – Gospel of Thomas, saying 18

The disciples said to Jesus, 'Tell us in what way our end will be.' Jesus said, 'Have you therefore discerned the beginning since you seek after the end? For in the place where the beginning is, there will be the end. Happy is he who will stand boldly at the beginning, he shall know the end, and shall find Life independent of death.'

SOURCE Q – *Circles*

> Within the circles of our lives
>   we dance the circles of the years;
>   the circles of the seasons
>   within the circles of the years;
>   the cycles of the moon
>   within the circles of the seasons;
>   the circles of our reasons
>   within the cycles of the moon.
>
> Again and again
>   we come and go;
>   changed . . .
> *Wendell Berry*

SESSION 5 – RENDING THE VEIL

Meeting outline for Session 5

Welcome

Opening worship (see page 33)

Silence

Group exploration

▸ Given Jesus' attitude to the Law in Source F, what was the significance of the veil tearing from the top to the bottom at the moment of his death? (Sources R, S and T).

▸ It has been said that since the rending of the veil on Good Friday the church has spent 2000 years carefully sewing it up again. What is the group's understanding of this and what justification is there for that statement?

▸ How was the veil lifted for Brandub in Source U and how does this compare with the experience of others at the crucifixion?

Feedback from group exploration

Silence

Other activity

▸ Song, poem, video clip, drama or visual material relevant to this session.

Individual or paired reflection

▸ What are the veils that may be preventing your own transformation on a spiritual, emotional or physical level?

▸ What do you want to do about this? Who or what may stand in your way?

Feedback from reflection

Silence

Closing worship (see page 34)

SOURCE R – Mark 15:33-39

About midday the whole land became dark and stayed dark for three hours. About three o'clock, Jesus called out loud, 'Eloi, Eloi, lama sabachthani?' That means, 'My God, my God, why have you left me alone?' Some of the people standing there heard what Jesus said. They said, 'Listen, he is calling for Elijah!' One man ran to get something called a sponge. He made it wet with sour wine and put it on the end of a stick. With it he gave Jesus a drink. He said, 'We will see if Elijah will come and take him down!' Then Jesus called out loud. Then he died. The big cloth [i.e. veil] that hung in the temple was torn into two pieces. It was torn from the top down to the bottom. The captain who stood in front of Jesus saw that he died. He said, 'Surely, this man was God's Son.'

SOURCE S – Gospel of Thomas, saying 39

Jesus said, 'The Pharisees and the Scribes took the keys of Knowledge, and they hid them. Neither did they enter, nor did they allow those who wished to enter. But you, become prudent as serpents and innocent even as doves.'

SOURCE T – The temple and the veil

1 Kings 6 and Ezekiel 40, 41 and 42 contain much information about the construction of the temple in Jerusalem. Essentially, like most churches, it had three parts – the Ulam (the entrance), the Hekal (a large room for worship) and the Debir (the sanctuary). The Debir was also known as the Holy of Holies, the most sacred part of the complex, since it contained the Ark of the Covenant.

Every part of this room was covered in solid gold, and the Ark itself was guarded by huge flying figures carved from olive wood. The Ark was made of acacia wood, again covered in gold, which stood on a platform to keep it raised above floor level.

Very few men (and no women) were allowed in the Holy of Holies – this was reserved for a few very senior priests who were considered especially worthy and who were descendants of Zadok.

While the Jews were in exile, Exodus 36 tells us that: 'The Ark was protected by a curtain of blue, purple and scarlet yarn and finely twisted linen, with cherubim worked into it by a skilled craftsman. They made four posts of acacia wood for it and overlaid them with gold. They made gold hooks for them and cast their four silver bases. For the entrance to the tent they made a curtain of blue, purple and scarlet yarn and finely twisted linen – the work of an embroiderer; and they made five posts with hooks for them. They overlaid the tops of the posts and their bands with gold and made their five bases of bronze.'

It seems that this tradition of having a veil across the Debir was still maintained in the temple at the time of Jesus, and that it was this veil that was torn from top to bottom when Jesus died.

SOURCE U – St Kevin and the wild boar

One day a wild boar came running through the woods, panting with fright, and hid in Kevin's chapel. A few moments later a cruel huntsman called Brandub, notorious for killing both animals and humans merely for pleasure, arrived with a pack of snarling hounds. The hounds went up to the entrance of the chapel, but refused to go in, falling silent and bowing their heads. Brandub was on the point of yelling at the hounds, accusing them of cowardice, when he saw Kevin nearby, standing under a tree; birds were perched on Kevin's arms and were flying around his head, singing with joy. Then a wind arose, and the leaves in the tree became a chorus for the birds' song, rustling in perfect harmony. The cruel huntsman was filled with fear, and fell off his horse on to the ground. Then he crawled to Kevin and begged his blessing. From that day onwards Brandub never again killed people or animals, and lived instead on wild herbs.

Robert van de Weyer

*As we journey inward during this season
of transformation,
        may the peace and love
        of the Holy Three be with us.*

OPENING WORSHIP

Leader 1:   It's been a long, long day,
          and I've found too little time
          to recognise your presence.

   It's been a long, long day,
          and there's been too little quiet
          to hear you speak with me.

   It's been a long, long day,
          and I feel too tired
          to offer you the best of my abilities.

   It's been a long, long day,
          and I feel a long way
          from your love and security.

Leader 2:   In a time of silence
          let's reflect on how we are at this time:
          where we are with God,
          where we are with ourselves,
          where we are with each other.

   Let's reflect particularly on this past week
          and share with God the times when we have not
          lived up to expectations – God's – or our own

   Let's reflect on the times when we have not
          taken opportunities to further the kingdom,
          when we have not spoken out against injustice,
          when we have passed by on the other side

   (*Silence . . .*)

   We rest in the stillness of your being.
   We rest in the stillness of your love.
   We rest in the stillness of your reconciliation
          and the knowing that you alone can make us whole.

   A song may be sung

CLOSING WORSHIP

Leader 3: Into the love of the Holy Three
All: We place ourselves this night.

Leader 3: Into the care of the Holy Three
All: We place all that we have been,
    all that we are
    and all that we shall be.

Leader 3: Into the peace of the Holy Three
All: We place all those things
    that might trouble or disturb our rest . . .

Leader 3: . . . this and every night;
All: . . . this and every night.

Leader 3: In the name of the Creator,
    I ask a blessing of calm on us;

    In the name of the Son,
    I ask a blessing of peace on us;

    In the name of the Spirit,
    I ask a blessing of healing on us;

    In the name of the Holy Three,
    I ask these three blessings
      on us and those we love
      today
      every day
      each sleep
      each waking.

All: Amen.

BIBLIOGRAPHY AND SUGGESTIONS
FOR FURTHER READING

Adam, David	*A Desert in the Ocean – God's Call to Adventurous Living* (SPCK 2000)
Adam, David	*The Edge of Glory – Prayers in the Celtic Tradition* (SPCK 1985)
Adam, David	*Tides and Seasons – Modern Prayers in the Celtic Tradition* (SPCK 1989)
Baggott, Andy	*The Celtic Wheel of Life* (Gateway 2000)
Douglas-Klotz, Neil	*Prayers of the Cosmos – Meditations on the Aramaic Words of Jesus* (Harper 1990)
Douglas-Klotz, Neil	*The Hidden Gospel – Decoding the Spiritual Message of the Aramaic Jesus* (Quest Books 1999)
Kindred, Glennie	*Sacred Celebrations* (Gothic Image Publications 2001)
Kindred, Glennie	*The Earth's Cycle of Celebration* (Glennie Kindred 1991)
Mitton, Michael	*Restoring the Woven Cord* (DLT 1995)
Rosa Romani	*Green Spirituality* (Green Magic 2004)
Hugh McGregor Ross	*Jesus Untouched by the Church* (Sessions 1998)
Robert van de Weyer	*Celtic Fire* (DLT 1990)
Ken Wilber	*One Taste* (Shambhala 2000)

* *Indicates books that have been used as the principal sources for this course. All the books listed, however, are relevant to the wider issues of transformation and the Celtic way.*

Searching the Internet can be fascinating. There are many sites that discuss aspects of transformation, from a Christian and other points of view; many are very creative in their thinking!